YES I HAVE SOFTBALL FEVER DEAL. WITH. IT

Consumer Use Disclaimer: The "Yes I Have" book series was created in light-hearted, relatable fun to create distractions from things individuals may be dealing with. All "Yes I Have" books are not intended to diagnose medical conditions nor provide a cure for any medical conditions. This book is not meant to be a replacement for real medical intervention if needed.

ISBN: 978-1-958083-10-9

First Edition: April 2022

Yes I Have Anxiety, Inc.
Grove, Ok 74345

ask alesca to
Can you ~~play~~ play I can do it with a broken
by TS

WHAT ARE YOU DEALING WITH?
WE GOT YOU!

Visit www.YesIHave.com for more books!

Do you have an idea for the next "Yes I Have®" book? Reach out to us through our website!

You might just see your idea in a future book!

What are you dealing with?

YES I HAVE® ____________________

Design a Cool Softball Uniform!

Write Meaningful Notes to Your Teammates all Over This Page.

HOMERUN BALL! Write the Date of the Day you Hit Your First Homerun.

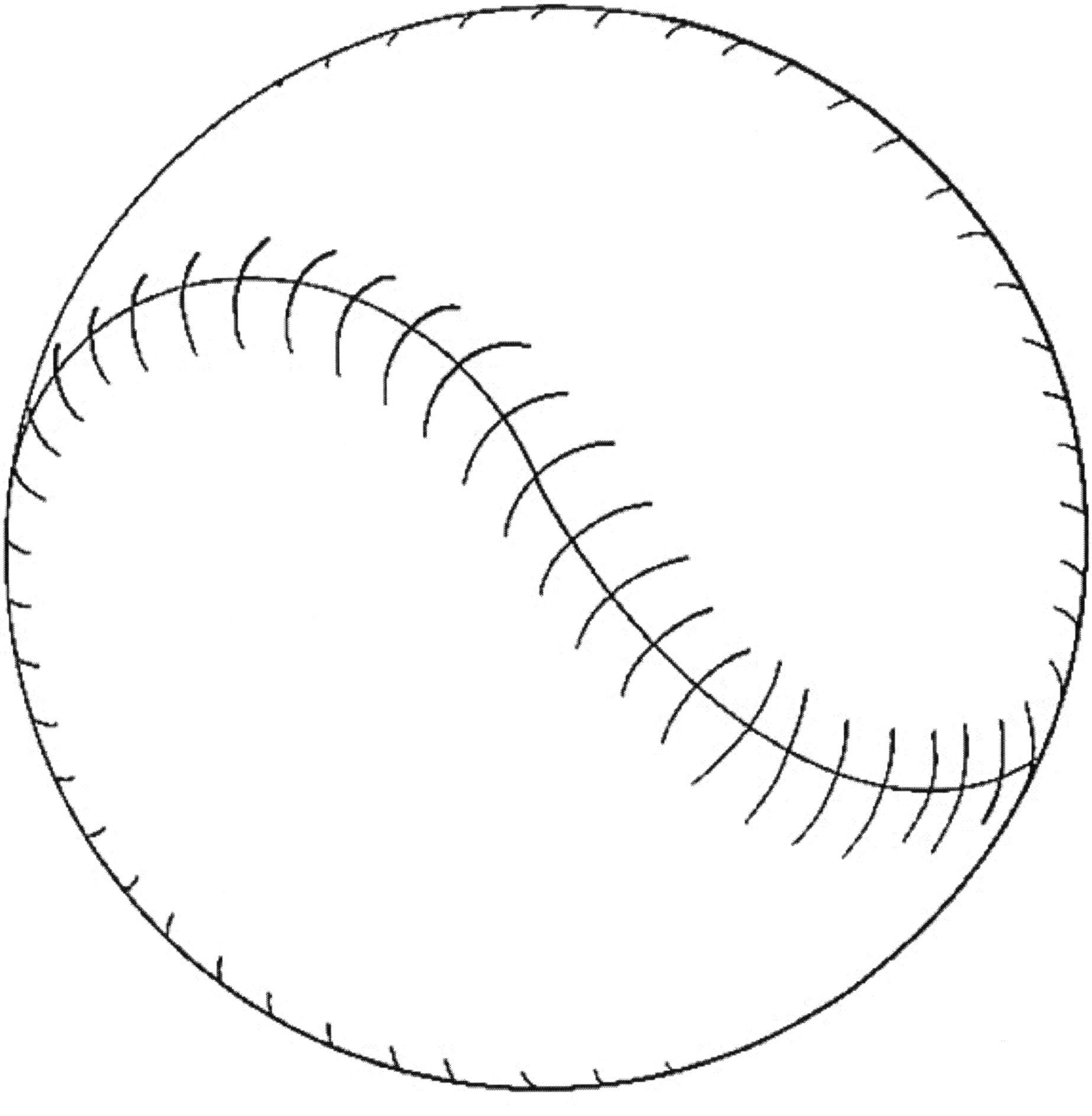

Decorate Your Facemask.

STATE TIME! Make Some State Send Off Posters.

What does Your Championship Trophy Look Like?

Tournament Time! What is on Your Packing List?

Design New Trading Pins for Your Team!

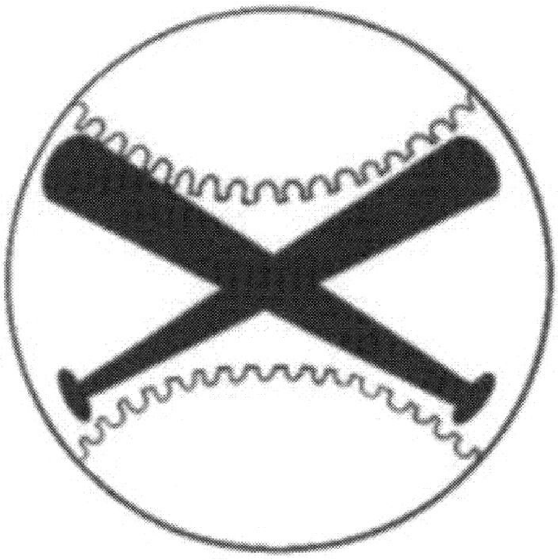

Gameday Hair! Make her Bow Stand Out.

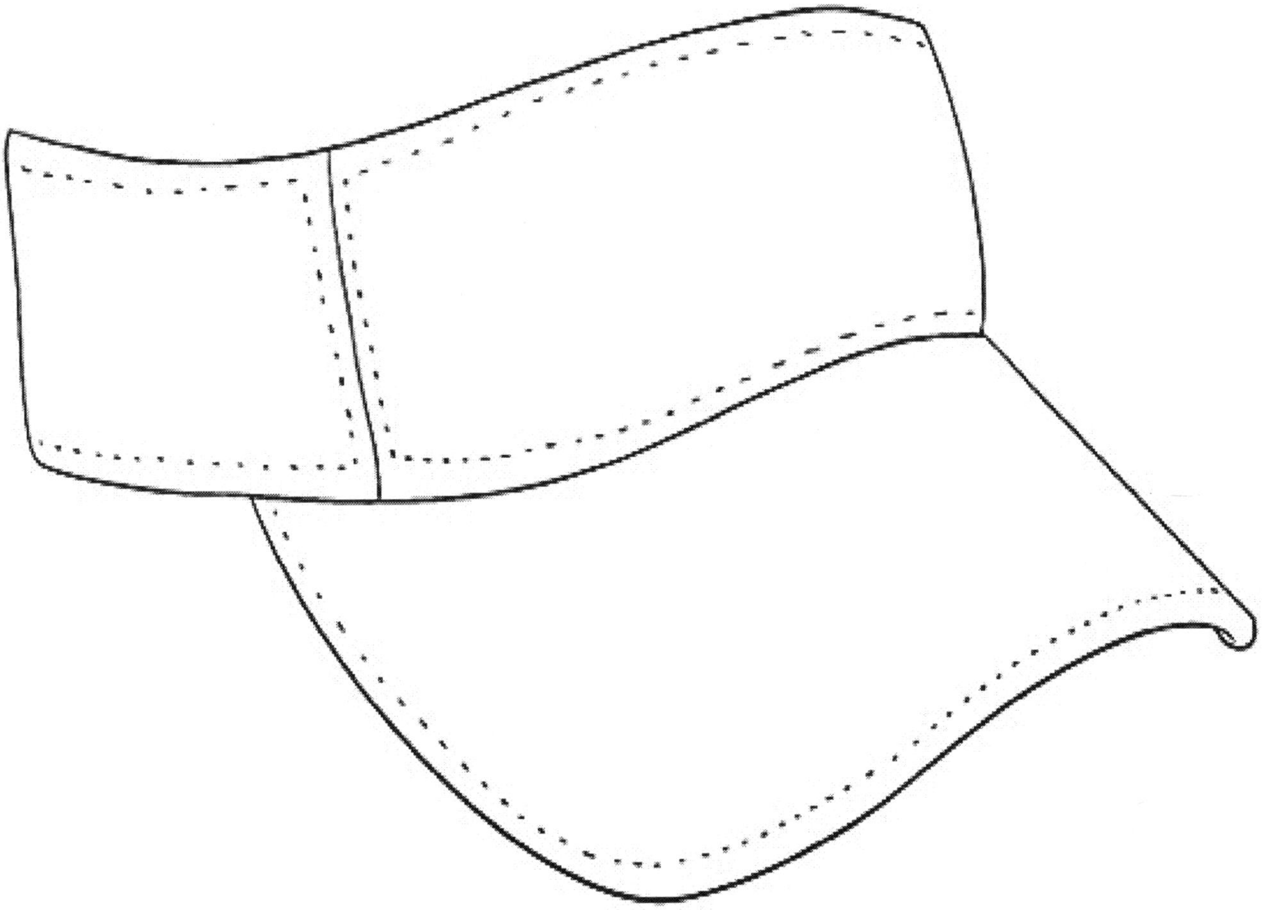

Make Your Visor Stand Out!

What are Your Favorite Team Bonding Activities?

Make a Cool Helmet and
Then an Ugly Helmet.

Design Your Championship Ring!

Draw Your Rival Mascot
and Then Black it Out.

Put Tags on the Suitcases With Your Favorite Softball Destinations.

Design Your Dream Glove!

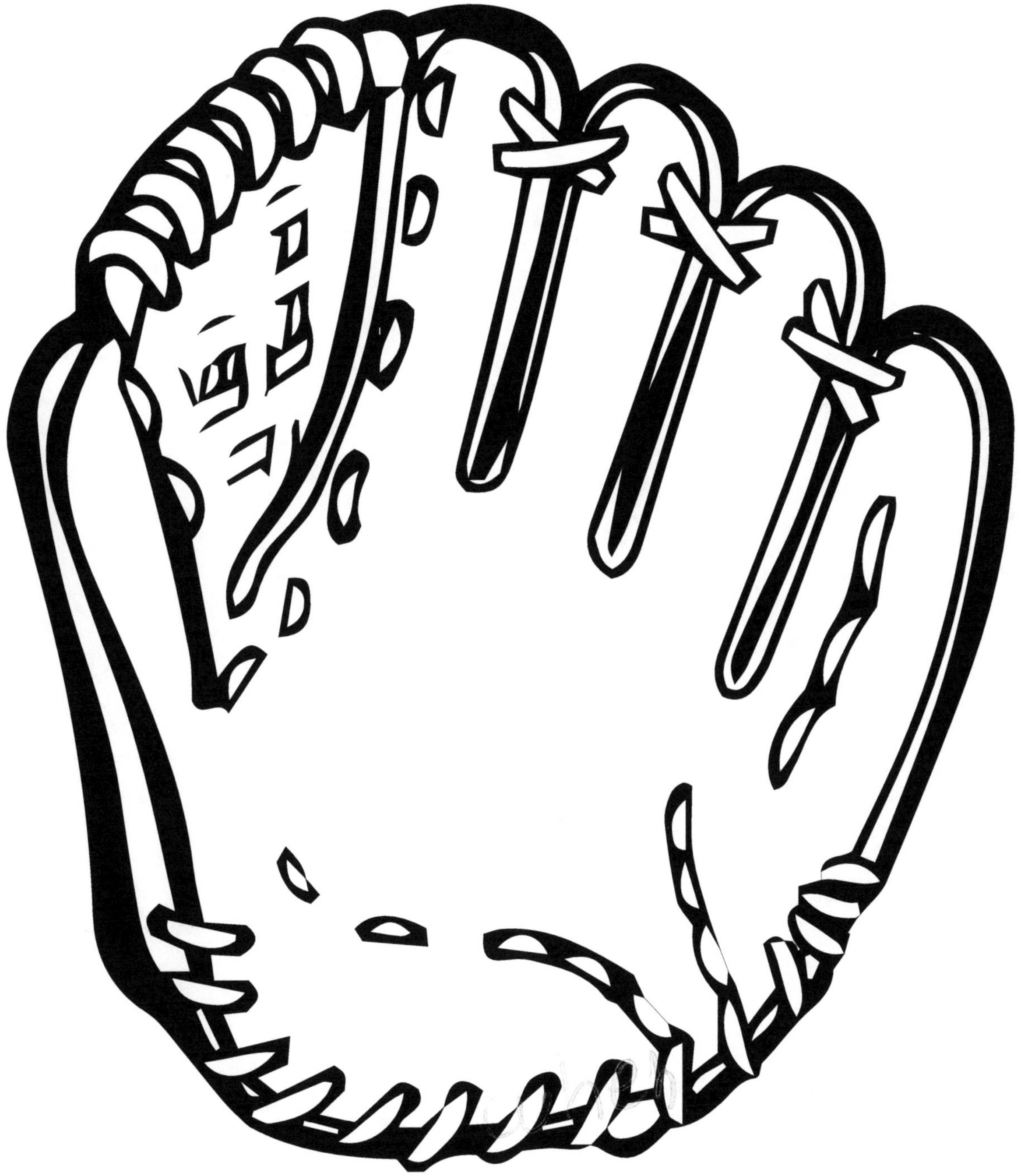

When we are learnig
we are changing roles.

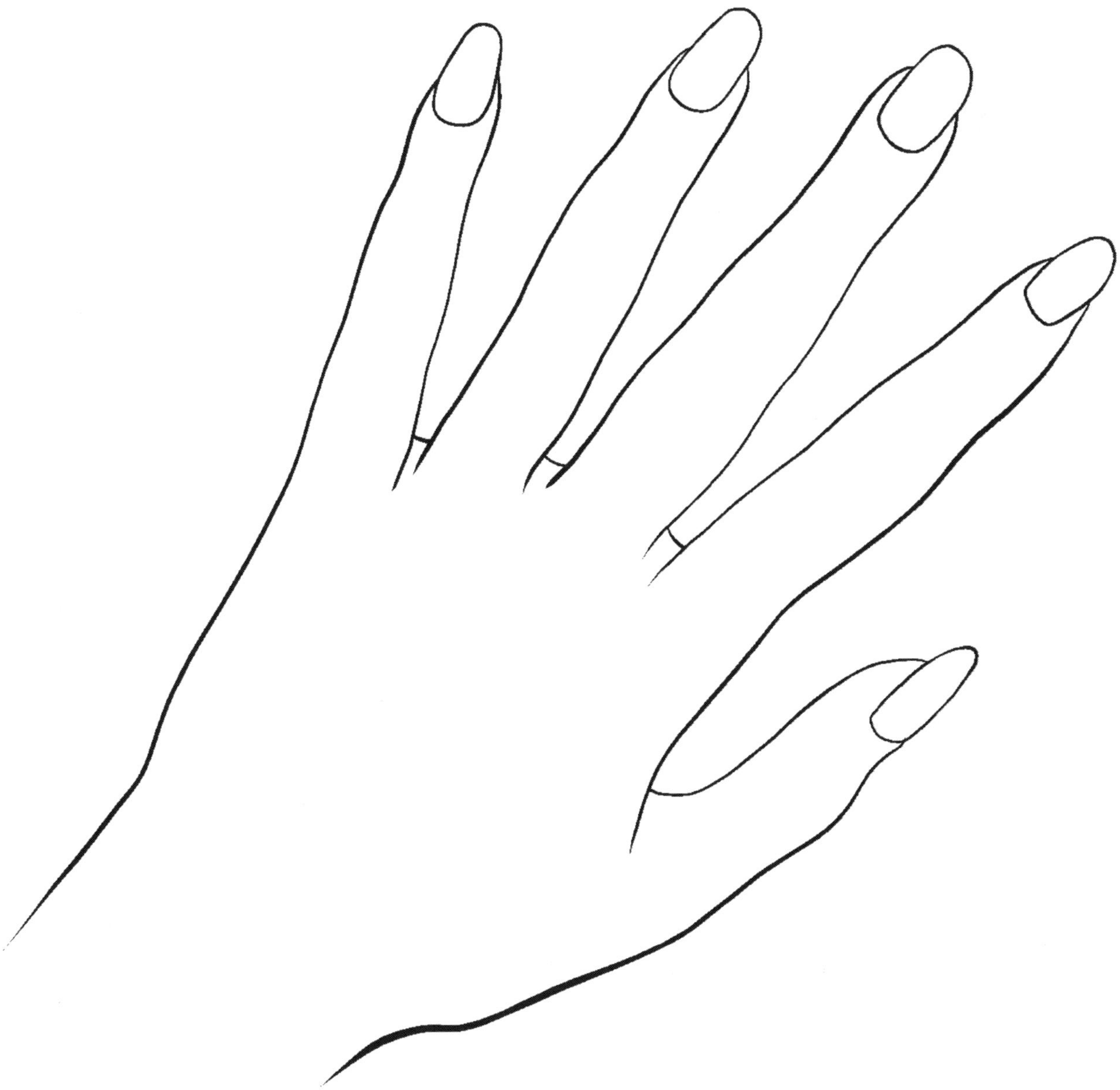

Paint Your Gameday Nails!

Make Your Cleats
Super Unique!

Spruce Up Your Headband!

Write Down All of Your Favorite
Pre-Game Chants!

Use the Mud from Your Cleats to
Paint a Picture on This Page!

How Many Softball Words can you Find?

C	T	R	I	P	L	E	C	A	T	C	H	E	R	N
C	G	R	S	T	R	I	K	E	O	U	T	D	R	S
Z	F	R	I	C	S	H	O	R	T	S	T	O	P	E
I	N	O	O	G	L	R	U	K	Y	T	I	U	C	C
T	L	F	R	U	H	E	U	E	T	M	U	B	C	O
U	H	I	I	C	N	T	A	N	W	U	B	L	L	N
N	B	I	N	R	E	D	F	T	D	E	P	E	P	D
I	U	A	R	E	S	O	B	I	S	O	W	S	I	B
F	N	H	L	D	D	T	U	A	E	H	W	I	T	A
O	T	O	P	L	B	R	B	T	L	L	V	N	C	S
R	G	M	O	R	S	A	I	A	F	L	D	G	H	E
M	L	E	P	A	O	G	S	V	S	M	O	L	E	C
T	O	R	F	N	S	X	L	E	E	E	U	E	R	F
A	V	U	L	L	E	F	T	F	I	E	L	D	D	V
G	E	N	Y	C	E	N	T	E	R	F	I	E	L	D

Design Your Catcher's Gear.

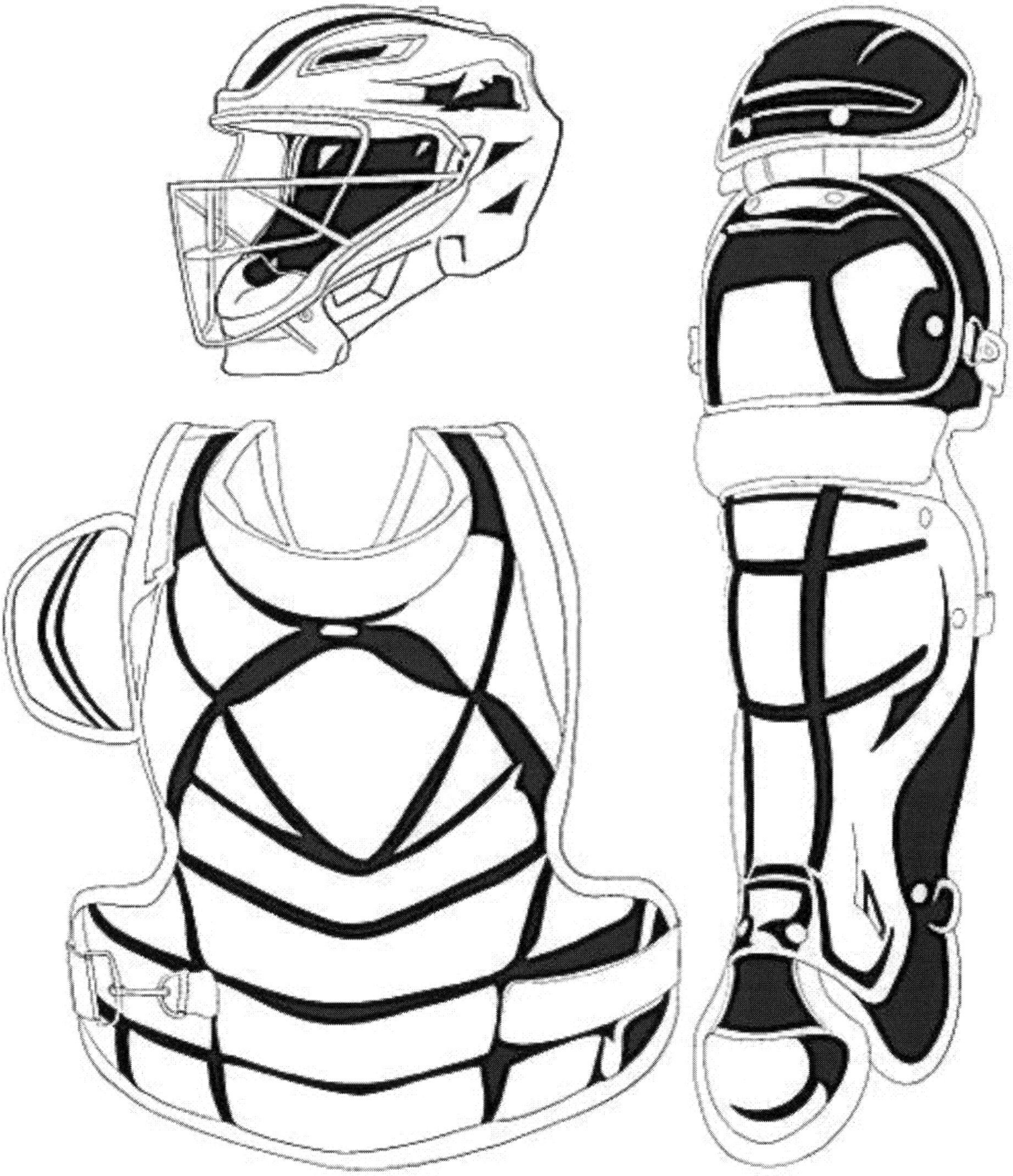

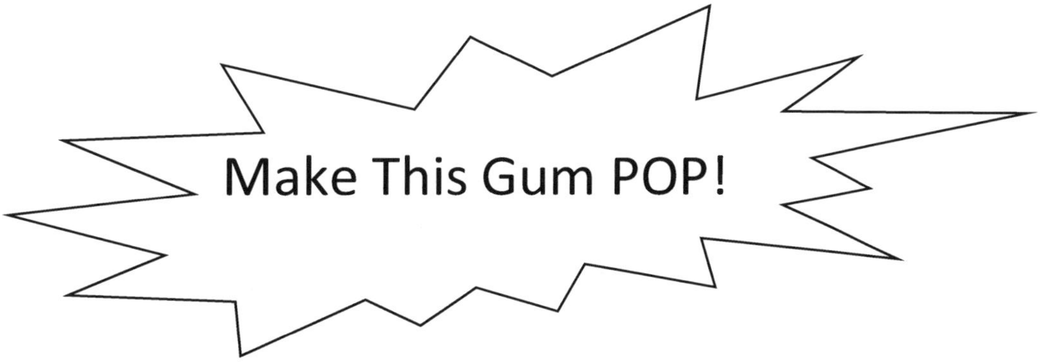
Make This Gum POP!

Glue your Favorite Snack
Wrappers to this Page.

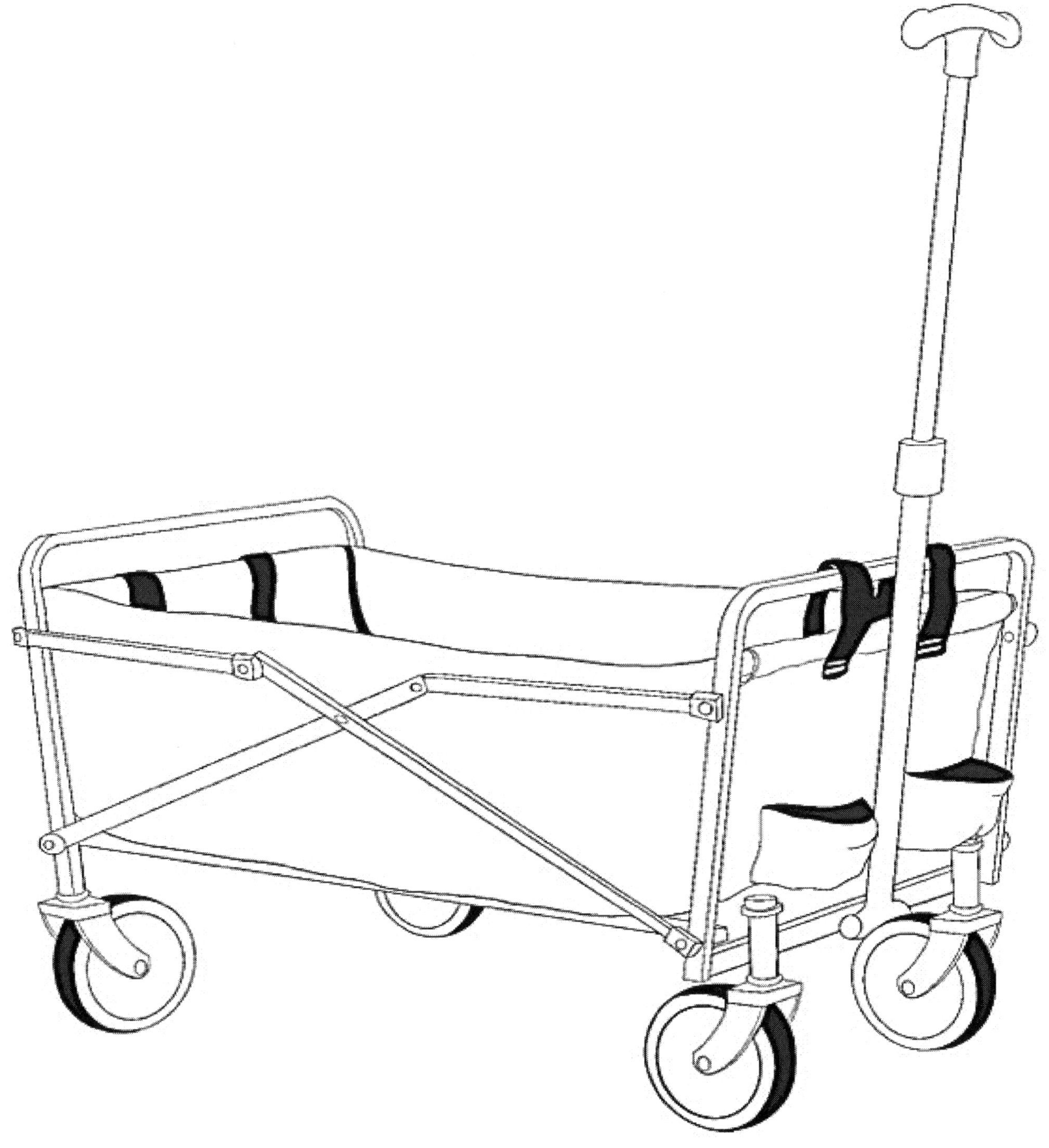

Pimp Out Your
Equipment Wagon!

Your Crush is Here! Make the Butterflies Go Away!

Turn the Circles into Softballs!

Clean Off the Dirt!

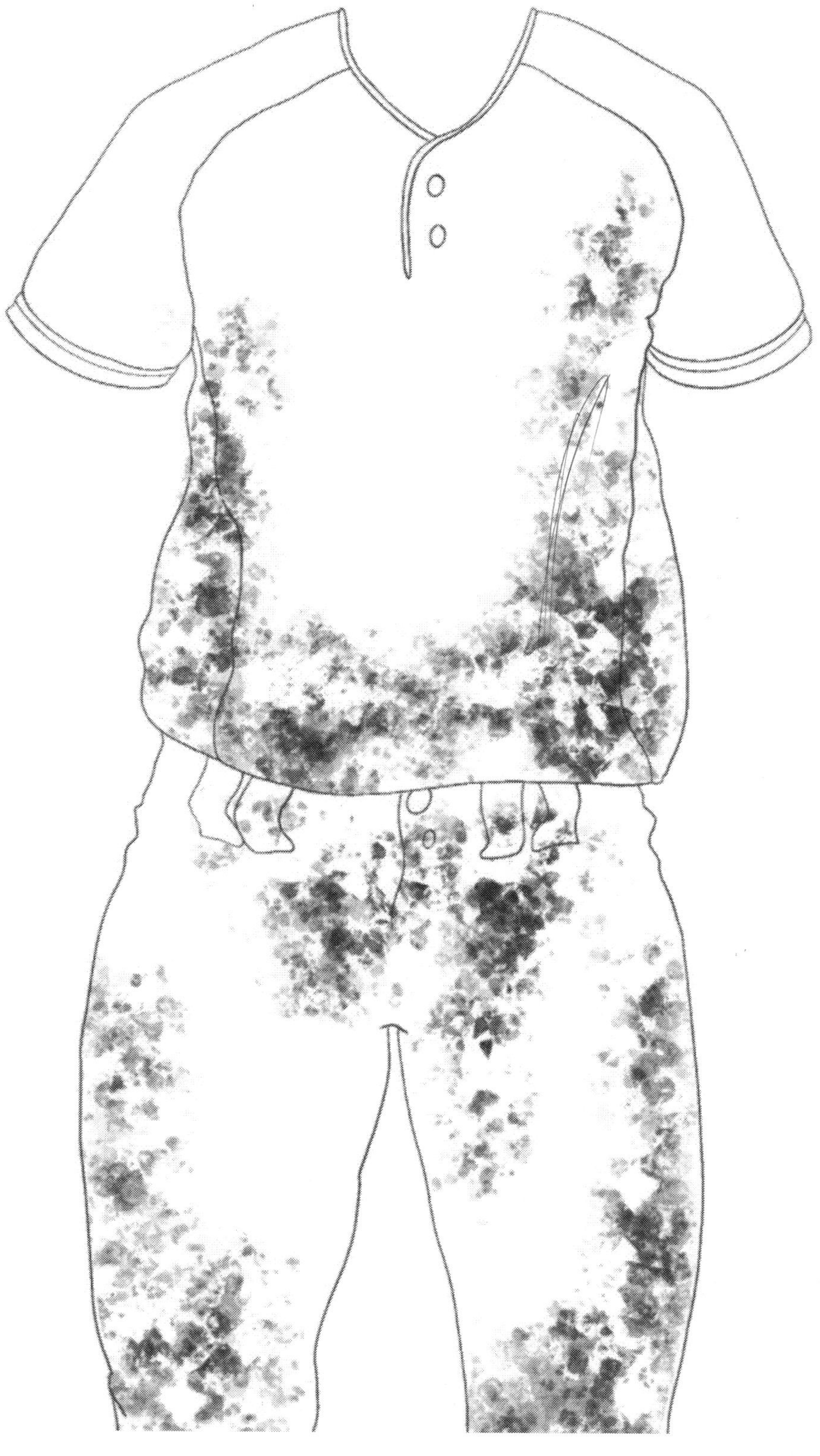

Create Your Own Lineup!

TEAM HAVOC 14U

Opponent vipers 14U Location Richmond Date 1-2-23

Order	NO.	Player	Position	NO.	Substitutes
1	10	Natalie	CF		
2	7	Kendall	s/t		
3	6	Evelym	Pitcher		
4	8	Addison	3rd		
5	5	JULia	Lf		
6	14	Gianna	fb		
7	24	Ally	catcher		
8	~~27~~	~~Tru~~			
9					
10					
11					
12					
13					
14					
15					
16					
17					

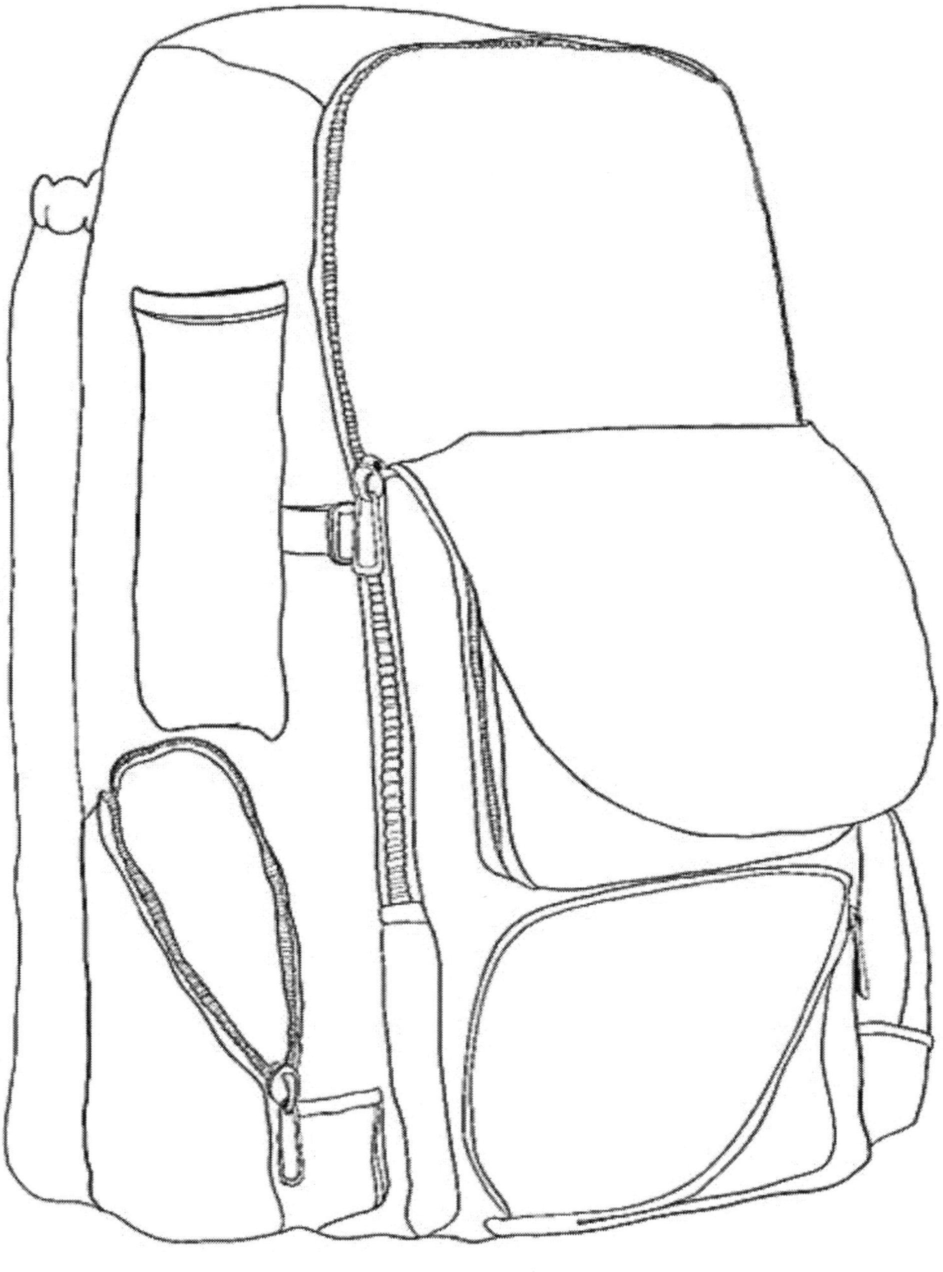

Decorate Your Softball Bag and Fill it
With What You Carry.

Decorate Your Hacky Sacks.

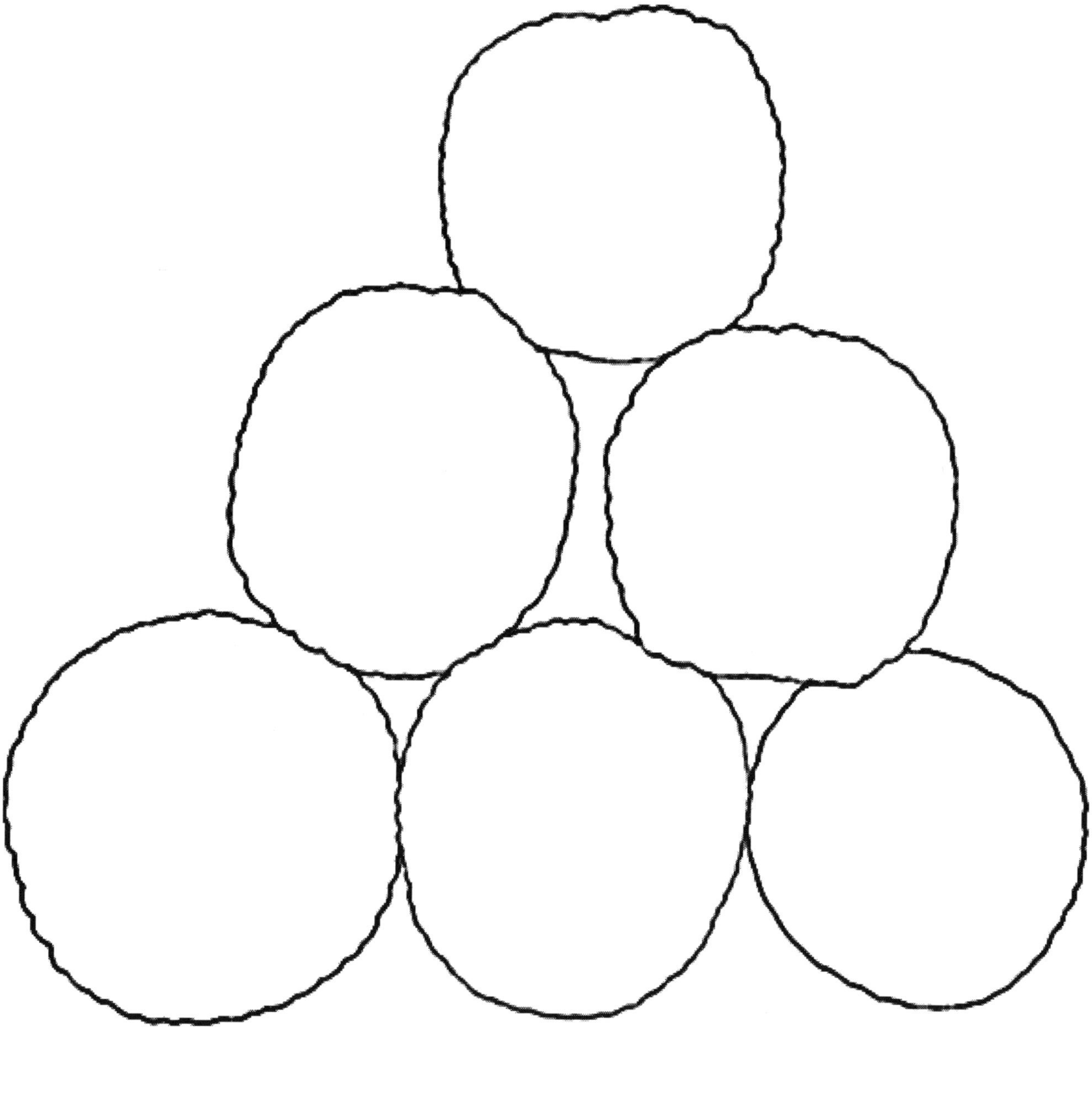

Write Your Favorite Inspirational Quotes All Over This Page.

What Teams Have you Played for or Found Inspiration From to Build Your Foundation?

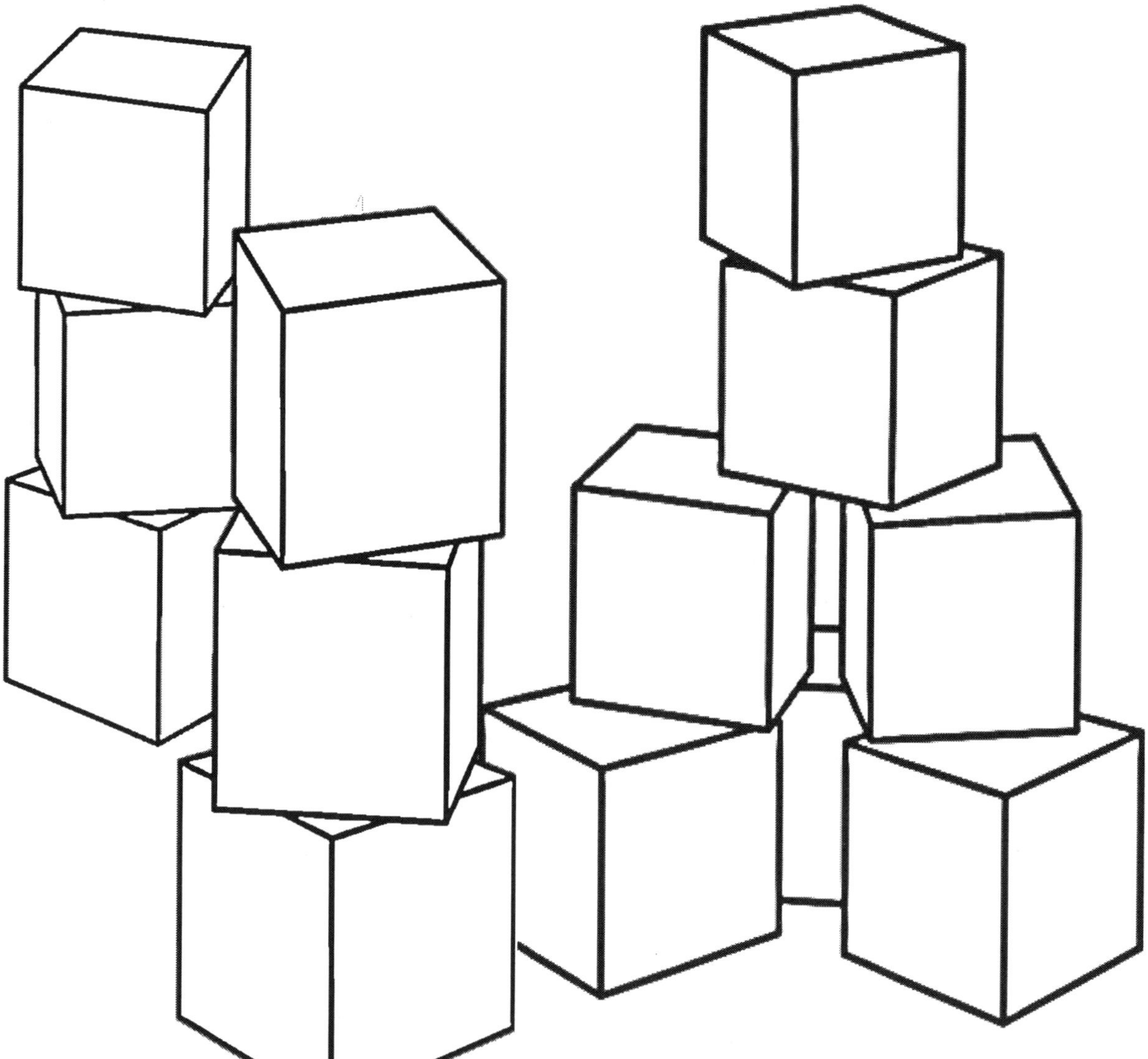

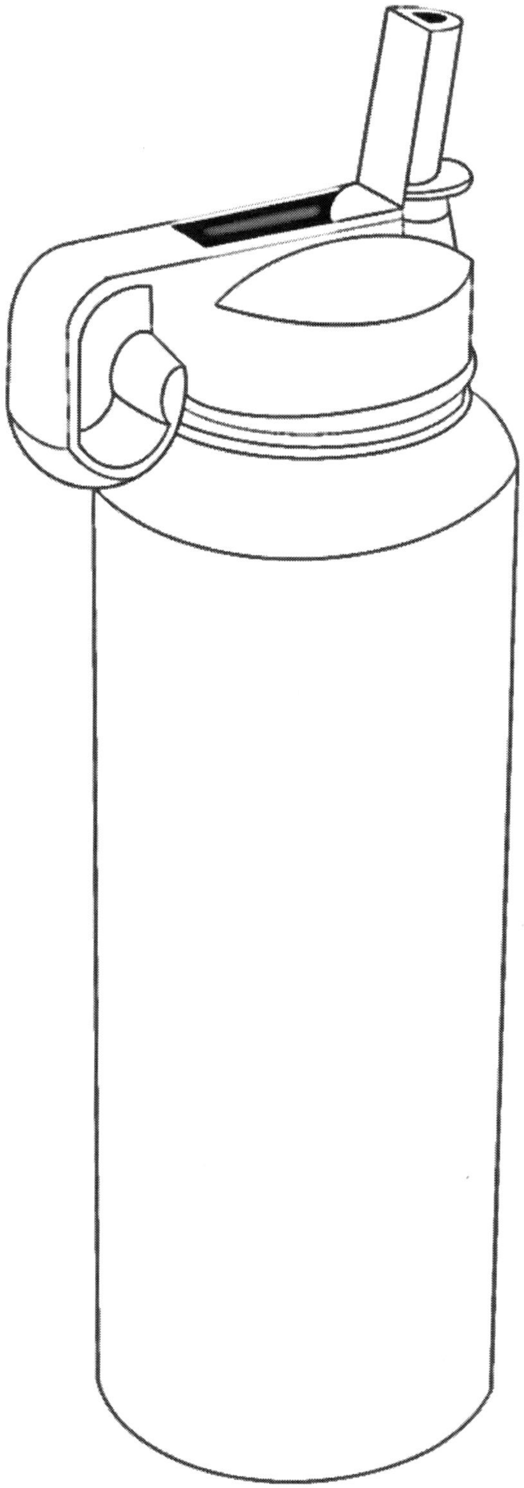

Decorate Your Practice Water Bottle!

Are Rainbow Sunflower
Seeds a Thing?

Game Break! Paint Your Favorite Restaurant Logo With a Fork and Spoon.

Add Spikes to the Cleats.

What does Your Coach Repeat
Too Many Times?
Write it All Over the Page.

Give Your Energy Drink
Some Energy!

You Sucked Today.

How are you Feeling Emojis?

Write the Lyrics to Your Favorite Warm Up Song!

Bedazzle Your Softball bat.

Glue Pictures of Your Favorite Team Memories.

You Just Hit a Walk Off to Win Nationals! CELEBRATE!

Cover This Entire Page with Real or Fake Popcorn!

Add Some Color to This Field and Make it Come to Life!

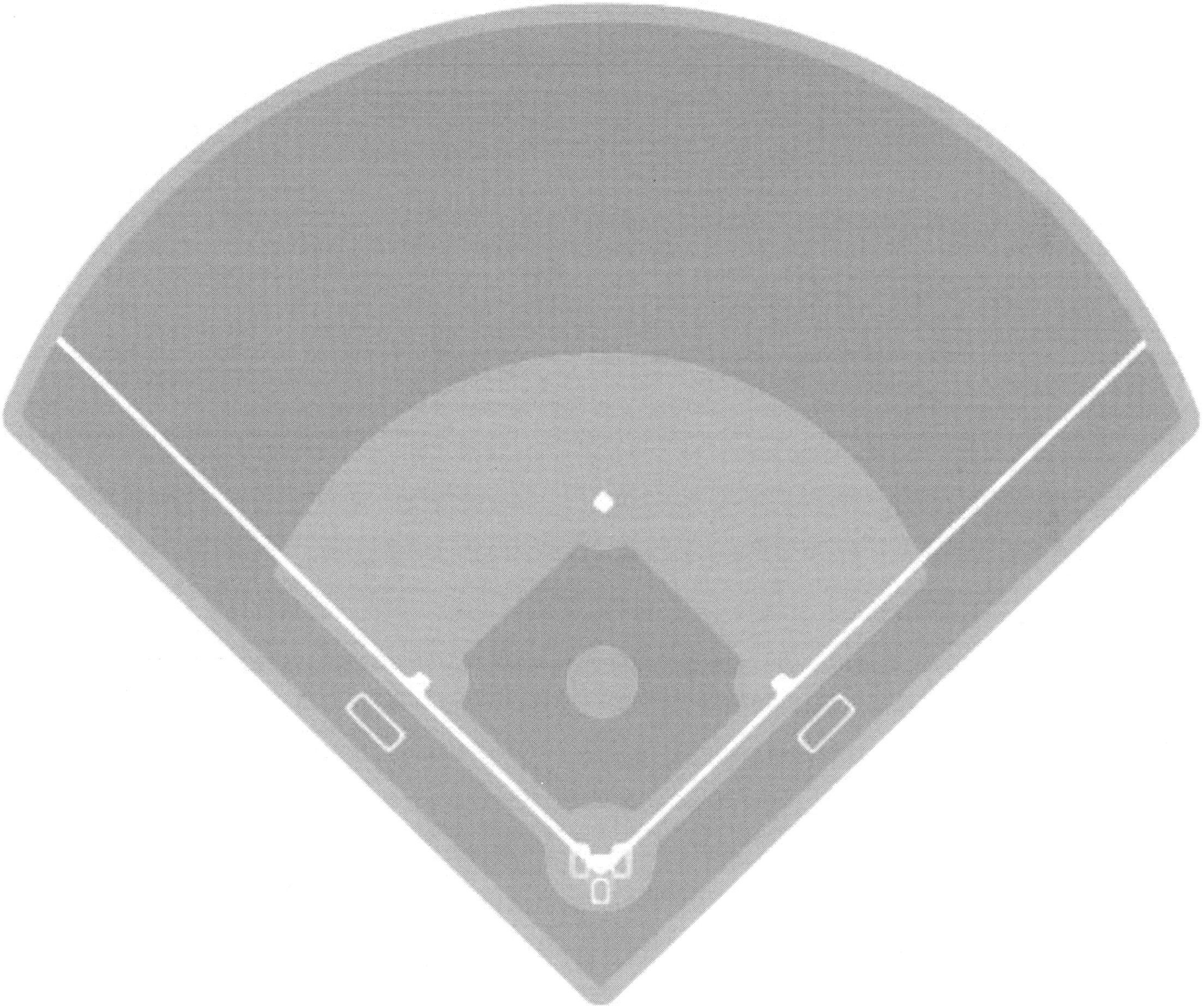

Compare Softball and Baseball!

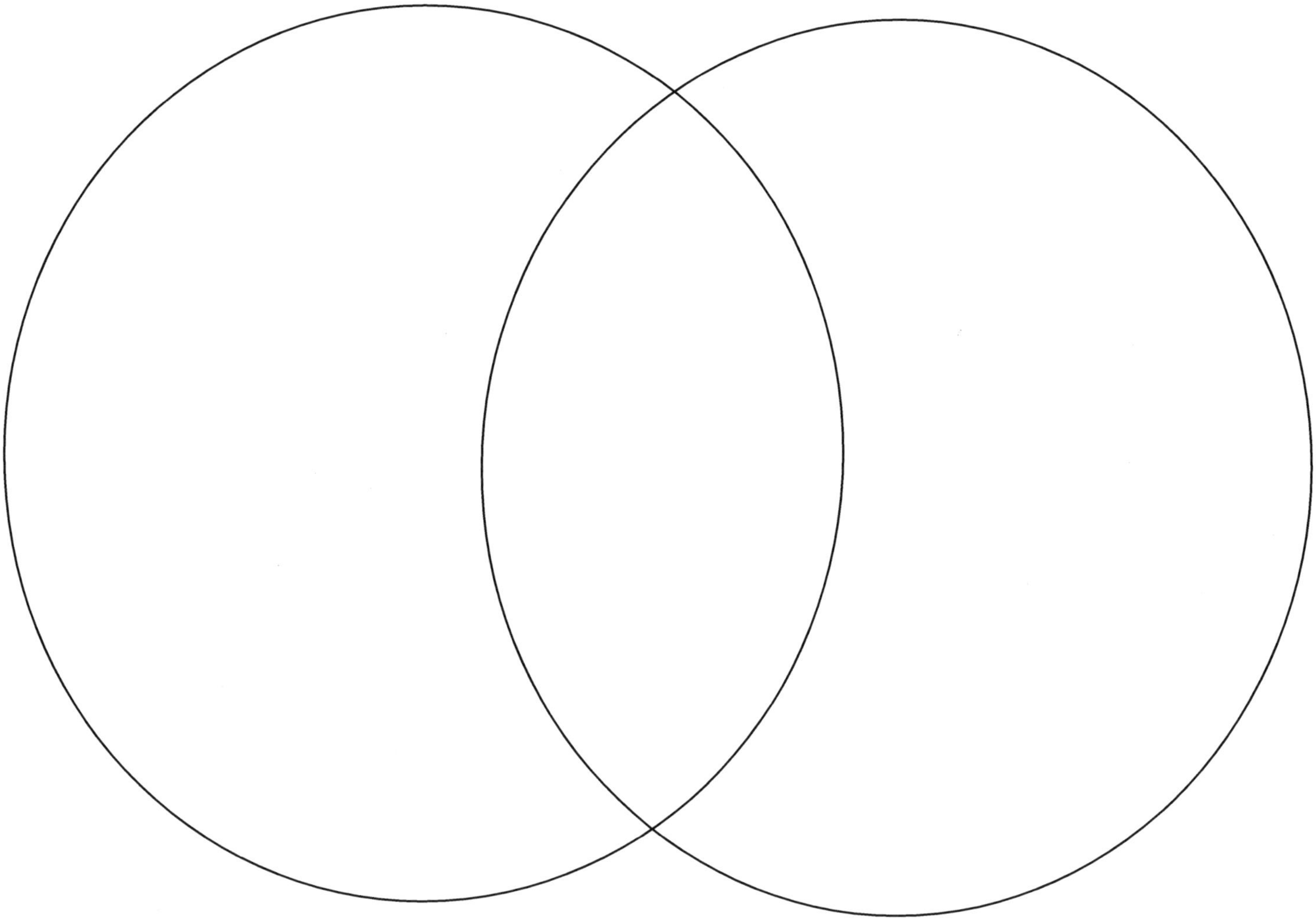

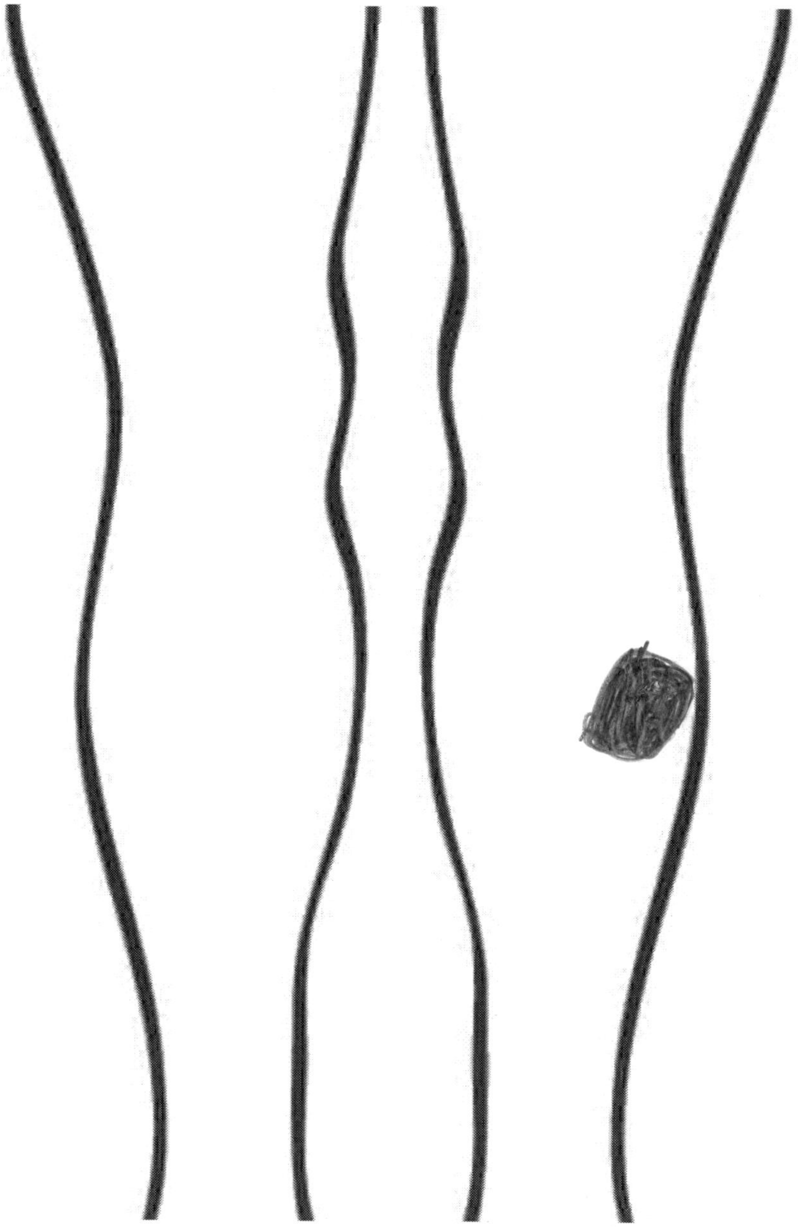

Softballs are NOT Soft. Add Bruises to the Legs.

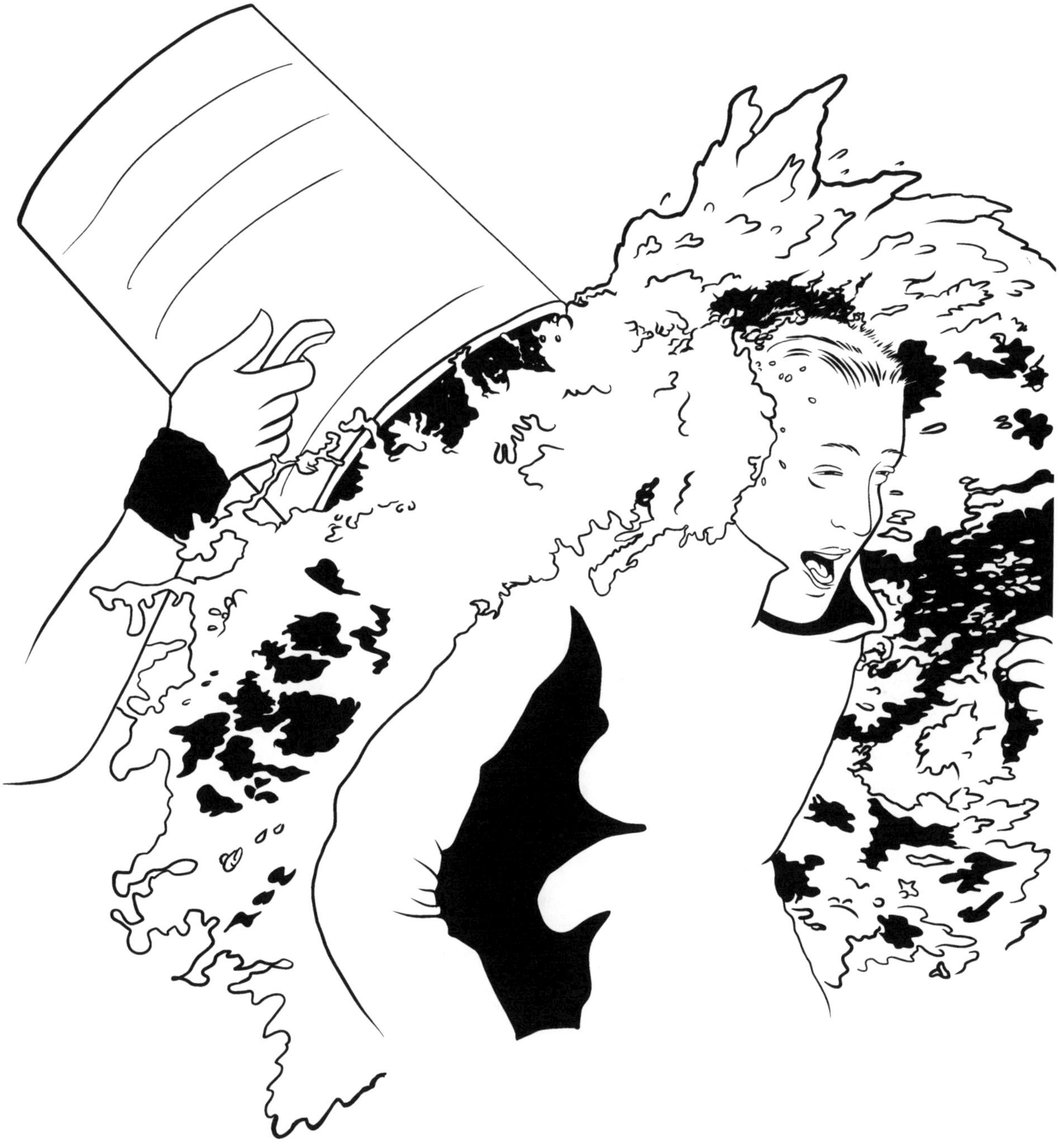

YOU WON STATE! Dump the Jug on Your Coach.

Don't miss out on FREE books and New Book Announcements!!!

Follow us on our social media platforms to be included in weekly giveaways, book tour location announcements, new book releases, and videos for page idea inspiration!!!

Instagram	TikTok	Facebook	YouTube
officialyesihave	yesihaveofficial	Yes I Have Books	Yes I Have Official

JOIN OUR NEWSLETTER!:

Text

YESIHAVE

To 22828 to get started!

Made in the USA
Middletown, DE
13 December 2022

18377906R00062